pestos,
tapenades
& spreads

pestos,
tapenades
& spreads

40 Simple Recipes for
Delicious Toppings, Sauces & Dips

by **Stacey Printz**
Photographs by Mark Lund

CHRONICLE BOOKS
SAN FRANCISCO

Library of Congress Cataloging-in-Publication Data available.

ISBN 978-0-8118-6589-0

Manufactured in China.

Prop styling by James Leland Day
Food styling by Liza Jernow
Designed by Jen Orth

10 9 8 7 6 5 4 3 2 1

Chronicle Books LLC
680 Second Street
San Francisco, California 94107

www.chroniclebooks.com

for Shawn and Bode—always.

There are some very important people who helped make this book possible. My deepest thanks to:

- *Amy Treadwell*
  for believing in this book from the beginning.

- *Sarah Billingsley*
  for seeing the project through with a fresh outlook
  and creative vision.

- The Chronicle team, including:
  *Jacob Gardner, David Hawk, Ben Kusman, Bill LeBlond,
  Mark Lund, Doug Ogan & Peter Perez.*

- *Elaine Printz & Staci Ann Printz,*
  testers I could count on.

- *Thank you to my family & friends*
  for everything. Especially to Mom for introducing
  me to the joys of cooking.

- *I offer special thanks to my husband*
  for his endless support and for always making me
  feel as if I can do anything.

- *And, finally, to my new little boy*
  for being the light that I never knew I was missing.

introduction 8

a word about ingredients 12

pestos 14

tapenades 38

spreads 68

introduction

Whether entertaining friends or cooking for our families, many of us desire delicious food with little fuss but tons of flavor. If you're like me, with a busy schedule and one too many things on your to-do list, you will agree that it's difficult to find the time for elaborate and complex preparations and recipes. At our favorite restaurants, it's often the rich, savory mixtures topping our appetizers and entrées that tempt our palates the most. I have discovered that I can blend up a pesto, tapenade, or spread and add a rich, vibrant punch to almost any dish, giving me that same

high-quality, mouth-watering restaurant meal I crave, all without investing tons of time. With that in mind, I created recipes that don't involve many steps or ingredients, yet achieve real flavor—recipes with the ability to transform everyday foods into sumptuous creations.

In *Pestos, Tapenades & Spreads,* I offer recipes that use fresh ingredients to make unique toppings. Each recipe includes multiple serving suggestions, so you'll get a lot of mileage out of each one. They last for many days in the refrigerator, so you can make one recipe and use it to top crostini for a festive Saturday night cocktail party, then use leftovers in a sauté with shrimp for your family's Monday night dinner. These recipes can be made ahead of time, and many of them get better the longer the flavors meld. Cooking chicken for an impromptu Sunday night meal with your in-laws? Top it with the Feta-Mint tapenade, and suddenly you have a real dazzler that's reminiscent of a Mediterranean *fattoush* salad. When I am eager to see friends, throwing a last-minute get-together is just the answer. However, I want to spend my valuable time catching up with them, not doing excess work in the kitchen. That's when recipes like the Edamame Hummus are great. Serve it with crudités or cooked shrimp for dipping, or spread it over crostini topped with sliced seared ahi.

This book is divided into three categories

based on texture and primary ingredients, and each chapter includes diverse flavor profiles. I wrote this with stress-free cooking in mind, leaving plenty of room for your own personal panache, so I encourage you to be loose and comfortable with measurements and cooking style. Play with quantities and serving ideas based on your personal preferences; don't be afraid to make substitutions. Do you prefer a little more lemon? Do you like extra cheese or more honey? Go for it!

These tasty accompaniments are your

ticket to turning plain chicken into a flavor-packed entrée or average appetizers into instant crowd-pleasers. Why eat "naked food" when you can easily jazz it up with a simple topping? Whether you're using them as dips, condiments, sauces or simply slathering them on warm bread, these stylish recipes will always delight.

a word about ingredients

The following is a list of some core ingredients (with tips for storage and usage) that are useful to have on hand for many of the recipes in this book.

fresh herbs: Fresh ingredients can really make a world of difference in your cooking. The vivid, pure flavors allow for a much greater impact on the palate. If you do not have the space or time for growing your own fresh herbs, many farmers' markets and grocery stores sell a wide variety. The recipes will indicate whether an alternative dried herb can be used.

> tip: Store basil and other soft-leaved herbs such as cilantro and parsley like a bouquet of flowers in a jar or vase of water on the countertop. Store woody herbs in the refrigerator in a plastic bag with a dry paper towel. They should be loose rather than tightly packed to prevent bruising and to help keep them fresh longer.

kalamata olives: These olives have a rich, salty flavor that lend themselves perfectly to many tapenade recipes. Some recipes will call for other varieties, but when in doubt, go with kalamata olives. They're a good choice to keep on hand in the pantry for last-minute uses.

> tip: While I encourage experimentation and substitution in all of these recipes, when it comes to olives, plain black olives are not a great alternative unless they are specified. Niçoise, Nyon, or Gaeta olives are good swaps. Different olives will impart different qualities to the dish—some more salty, some more mild or sweet. Play with finding your favorites for each recipe.

nuts: Many of the pesto recipes call for nuts. The most common are walnuts and pine nuts, but you will also see pistachios, cashews, peanuts, and several others. Often there are a few choices that will work with a given recipe.

> tip: Nuts can go rancid easily, so always taste a few from the bag prior to adding them to the food processor. For longevity, store extra nuts in an airtight container away from heat and light or, better yet, put them in the refrigerator or freezer.

olive oil: Extra-virgin olive oil will give you the best results in these recipes, but feel free to use what you have on hand. Olive oil can range in taste and price. So, while standard olive oils will do just fine, play with incorporating different styles of olive oil that are available—from slightly herbaceous and full bodied to earthy, rich, and buttery.

> tip: Oil can go rancid, so always smell your oil before using it in a recipe. Your nose will let you know if it has gone bad!

other key ingredients

- balsamic vinegar
- cream cheese
- garlic
- lemon
- onion
- Parmesan cheese

pestos

Sweet and mild basil, clean cilantro, earthy sage, or zingy mint are core ingredients in this chapter. It's all about fresh herbs! Mixing up a batch of pesto is an easy and flavorful way to add vibrancy to any meal. Tantalizing the taste buds with fresh herbs adds spark to an otherwise casual dinner or appetizer. Pesto, from the Italian word *pestare* (meaning "to pound" or "to crush"), in its traditional form consists of a purée of basil, olive oil, garlic, pine nuts, and Parmesan cheese. These days, "pesto" is also used to describe similar emulsified mixtures that contain other herbs or nuts. In its many forms, pesto can be a tasty topping for pastas, chicken, meat, and fish.

The pestos in this book will last for a week or two in the refrigerator or can easily be stored in the freezer for three months. Pouring a thin layer of olive oil over pesto before putting it in an airtight container in the refrigerator helps to preserve the pesto by inhibiting browning and spoilage. Try spooning the pesto into ice cube trays and, once frozen, pop the pesto cubes into a zip-top bag. Then you can use one or two cubes whenever the mood strikes. As you will see, these are versatile recipes that will really enhance your cooking in a flash.

traditional basil

This is a great recipe during the summer when basil is plentiful. Garden-fresh basil is one of my favorite parts of the warm, sunny months, and this pesto is so adaptable, you will find that it easily fits into any outdoor barbeque.

2 1/2 cups of packed fresh basil leaves

1 large or 2 small garlic cloves, minced

3/4 cup grated Parmesan cheese

1/2 cup pine nuts or walnut pieces

Salt and freshly ground pepper

1/2 cup good-quality extra-virgin olive oil

Place the basil, garlic, cheese, and nuts in the bowl of a food processor, season with salt and pepper, and blend until a coarse mixture forms. With the machine running, gradually stream in the olive oil and blend until the pesto has emulsified.

makes about 1 cup

serving suggestions

- Toss pasta with the pesto and garnish with chopped fresh tomatoes or add sautéed zucchini and/or Italian sausage.
- Place a spoonful atop grilled fish.
- Pound chicken breasts, dust with flour or bread crumbs, and sauté. Top with the pesto and fresh tomatoes and serve over hearty greens, such as a mixture of arugula and spinach.
- Mix into mashed potatoes for added flavor and color.
- Serve on grilled bread with fresh tomatoes.

no-nut

Because my nephew is allergic to nuts, I promised my sister-in-law that I would develop a pesto he could eat. It's just as tasty as the original and can be used like traditional pesto. The croutons make this version perfect for creating a pesto crust on fish or chicken.

2 cups packed fresh basil leaves
½ cup grated Parmesan cheese
⅔ cup croutons (fresh artisan style are best)
1 garlic clove, minced
½ cup olive oil
Salt and freshly ground pepper (optional)

Place the basil, cheese, croutons, and garlic in the bowl of a food processor and pulse until a coarse crumb mixture forms. With the machine running, gradually stream in the olive oil and blend until the pesto emulsifies. Season with salt and pepper, if using.

makes about 1 cup

serving suggestions

- Use to encrust chicken or fish. Pat onto the chicken or fish and bake.
- Toss with your favorite pasta and 2 tablespoons of olive oil. Add a squeeze of lemon juice.
- Add a dollop to vegetable soup.
- Layer on crostini with chopped, seeded tomatoes and/or shaved Parmesan cheese.

green pea

This cheerfully colored pesto tastes like spring with a bright and slightly sweet flavor. Peas are protein rich and low in fat, giving this recipe unexpected nutritional power.

2 ½ cups frozen peas

3 tablespoons olive oil

1 to 2 garlic cloves, minced

½ cup packed basil leaves

3 tablespoons pine nuts

3 tablespoons grated Parmesan cheese

Salt and freshly ground pepper

Cook the peas according to package instructions. Drain. Heat 1 tablespoon of the olive oil over medium heat. Sauté the peas and garlic until the garlic is fragrant, 1 to 2 minutes. Transfer the pea mixture to the bowl of a food processor. Add the basil, pine nuts, and cheese and pulse until a coarse paste forms. With the machine running, gradually stream in the remaining oil and blend until the pesto emulsifies and is almost smooth. Season with salt and pepper.

makes about 1 ⅔ cups

serving suggestions

- Spoon over ravioli topped with fresh crab or shrimp. Garnish with lemon zest, Parmesan cheese, and lemon wedges.
- Serve over grilled or baked salmon, halibut, or sea bass.
- Spread on crostini and top with a shaving of Parmesan cheese.

arugula

Also known as "rocket," arugula is a peppery, strong-tasting leafy green that is rich in vitamin C and iron. The strength, bitterness, and heat of arugula vary widely. For many people, the spicy notes are their favorite part of arugula, but if you like flavors a little milder, tone down an especially strapping batch by incorporating spinach leaves and/or adding more cheese.

2 garlic cloves, unpeeled

4 tablespoons olive oil

¼ cup pine nuts

3 cups packed arugula

¼ cup Pecorino Romano cheese

2 teaspoons fresh lemon juice

Salt

Place the garlic in a skillet with 1 tablespoon of the olive oil. Cook over medium-low heat until soft, 3 to 4 minutes. In another skillet, toast the pine nuts until lightly browned and fragrant. Peel and mince the garlic. Place the garlic, nuts, arugula, cheese, and lemon juice in the bowl of a food processor and pulse until a coarse paste forms. With the machine running, gradually stream in the remaining olive oil and blend until the pesto emulsifies. Season with salt.

makes ⅓–½ cup

serving suggestions

- Serve over a salad of fresh peaches and prosciutto (Italian ham).
- Toss with gnocchi, chopped fresh tomatoes, and shaved cheese.
- Make an arugula pesto pizza. Coat pizza dough with the pesto and mozzarella cheese and bake in a hot oven.

artichoke-lemon

This tangy pesto brings out the subtle flavor of the artichokes with a nice balance of acid from the lemons.

3 tablespoons olive oil
1/4 cup chopped white or yellow onion
1 garlic clove, minced
One 14-ounce can artichoke hearts in water,
    drained and quartered
2 tablespoons lemon juice
4 tablespoons grated Parmesan cheese
Salt and freshly ground pepper

Heat 1 tablespoon of the olive oil over medium-low heat. Sauté the onion and garlic until softened, about 3 minutes. Add the artichokes and continue to sauté for 2 to 3 more minutes. Transfer the mixture to the bowl of a food processor. Add the remaining oil, the lemon juice, and cheese. Season with salt and pepper and pulse until a coarse mixture forms. Do not overmix.

makes about 1 1/2 cups

serving suggestions

- Mound over any type of sautéed flaky white fish such as trout or cod. Garnish with chopped fresh parsley or thyme and serve with lemon wedges.
- Blanket crostini or fresh bread with the pesto and top with a shaving of Pecorino cheese and a sprinkle of chopped fresh parsley or thyme.
- Put a healthy tablespoon of this pesto under the skin of chicken breasts, top with additional pesto and Parmesan cheese, and bake.

cilantro

While cilantro looks similar to Italian parsley, the taste is quite different. Some call the flavor grassy and clean, while others say it's biting and tangy. However you describe it, it makes for a distinct and vivid pesto.

2 cups packed cilantro leaves
1/4 cup pine nuts, raw or toasted
1 large garlic clove, chopped
1/4 cup grated Parmesan cheese
3 tablespoons fresh lime juice
1/8 teaspoon salt
1/4 teaspoon freshly ground pepper
6 tablespoons olive oil

Place the cilantro, nuts, garlic, cheese, lime juice, salt, and pepper in the bowl of a food processor and blend until a coarse mixture forms. With the machine running, gradually stream in the oil and blend until the pesto emulsifies.

makes about 3/4 cup

serving suggestions

- Toss with grilled or sautéed shrimp.
- Toss with pasta, 3 tablespoons olive oil, and diced fresh red pepper.
- Stir into rice or risotto with corn kernels and *queso fresco* or other Mexican cheese.
- Use as a condiment for a grilled vegetable panini.
- Add to a stacked salad with thick slices of tomato, avocado, and *queso fresco*. Garnish with finely chopped red onion and/or chopped cilantro

thai

This recipe is an ode to the delicate blend of herbs and spices commonly found in Thai cuisine—in this case a blend of ginger, lime, and lemongrass. If you like your food hot, feel free to up the ante by adding more jalapeño.

> 1 cup packed fresh basil leaves
> 1/3 cup chopped cashews
> Zest from 1 lime
> Juice from 1/2 lime
> 1 teaspoon peeled and grated fresh ginger
> 1 to 2 jalapeño peppers, seeded and finely chopped
> 1 teaspoon soy sauce (dark or light)
> 1/4 teaspoon dried lemongrass
> 3 tablespoons olive oil

Place the basil, cashews, lime zest and juice, ginger, jalapeño, soy sauce, and lemongrass in the bowl of a food processor and pulse until a coarse mixture forms. With the machine running, gradually stream in the oil and blend until the pesto emulsifies.

makes about 3/4 cup

(serving suggestions, next page)

serving suggestions

- Toss with shrimp, 1 to 2 tablespoons of oil, your favorite Asian noodles (such as wheat, egg, ramen, or rice noodles), and sautéed mushrooms and onions.
- Add to any stir-fry.
- As an appetizer, serve wonton cups filled with seared fish that has been mixed with the pesto and garnish with ribbons of fresh basil. To make the wonton cups, preheat the oven to 350 degrees F. Brush wonton wrappers with a little melted butter, press them into the depressions of mini muffin tins and bake for 6 to 8 minutes, until lightly browned and crisp. Remove from the tins and let cool on wire racks.

rosemary

The woody, fragrant nature of rosemary is a great complement to robust foods. The powerful flavor stands up to even the boldest cuts of meat.

$1/4$ cup fresh rosemary

1 cup packed fresh parsley

2 garlic cloves, minced

$1/2$ cup walnuts

$1/2$ cup grated Parmesan cheese

6 tablespoons olive oil

Salt and freshly ground pepper

Place the rosemary, parsley, garlic, walnuts, and cheese in the bowl of a food processor and pulse until a coarse paste forms. With the machine running, gradually stream in the oil and blend until the pesto emulsifies. Season with salt and pepper.

makes 1 cup

serving suggestions

- Use as a thick rub for grilled chicken. Slather on chicken and grill over medium heat.
- Rub over lamb and roast in a hot oven.
- Lightly top broiled or grilled rib-eye steaks with this pesto.
- Toss with roasted potatoes during the last 10 minutes of cooking.

spinach

This is a great variation on the original basil pesto. It's also a sneaky way to get your kids to eat their spinach!

> 3 cups packed fresh spinach leaves, stems removed
> 1/4 cup pine nuts
> 1/3 cup freshly grated Parmesan cheese
> 1 to 2 garlic cloves, minced
> 1/4 teaspoon salt
> 1/3 cup olive oil
> Freshly ground pepper

Place the spinach, nuts, cheese, garlic, and salt in the bowl of a food processor and pulse until a coarse mixture forms. With the machine running, gradually stream in the oil and blend until the pesto emulsifies. Season with pepper.

makes about 1 cup

(serving suggestions, next page)

serving suggestions

- Season chicken breasts with salt and pepper. In an ovenproof skillet, sauté the chicken in olive oil until almost cooked through. Top with the pesto and shredded mozzarella cheese and place in the oven until the cheese is melted and the chicken is fully cooked.
- Serve over your favorite hot pasta.
- Pour over halved cherry tomatoes and sliced mozzarella cheese.
- Top crostini with the pesto, shaved Parmesan, and half of a cherry tomato or grape tomato.
- Stir into couscous or rice to add color and flavor.

sage-walnut

This wintry, rustic pesto is aromatic and full bodied. I serve it in the colder months to add vigor to seasonal recipes.

$1/2$ cup walnuts
$1/2$ cup packed fresh sage leaves
1 garlic clove, minced
$1/2$ cup extra-virgin olive oil
1 to 2 teaspoons balsamic vinegar
Salt and freshly ground black pepper

Place the walnuts, sage, garlic, oil, and vinegar in the bowl of a food processor, season with salt and pepper, and blend until almost smooth and the paste emulsifies.

makes about $1/2$ cup

serving suggestions

- Spread a thick layer of this pesto on boneless skinless chicken breasts and bake. During the last few minutes of baking, place a slice of provolone or Swiss cheese on top of each breast and return to the oven until melted.
- Incorporate into risotto: Prepare simple risotto or long-grain white rice and add a few tablespoons of the pesto during the last 5 minutes of cooking.
- Stir into your favorite stuffing for another layer of flavor.

mint-peanut

Refreshing mint and salty peanuts create a lively dance on the palate. Unlike most of the pestos in this book, this one only lasts for two to three days in the refrigerator before losing its vibrancy.

1 cup packed fresh basil leaves

3 tablespoons coarsely chopped fresh
    mint leaves

2 to 3 teaspoons peeled and grated fresh ginger

½ cup salted roasted peanuts

1 teaspoon sesame oil

Juice of 1 lime

4 tablespoons canola or vegetable oil

Salt and freshly ground pepper

Place the basil, mint, ginger, peanuts, sesame oil, lime juice, and canola oil in the bowl of a food processor. Season with salt and pepper and blend until almost smooth and the paste emulsifies. (If you only have unsalted peanuts on hand, simply add more salt.)

makes about ¾ cup

serving suggestions

- Toss with chopped napa or savoy cabbage, shredded carrots, chopped peanuts, and seasoned rice wine vinegar for a simple Asian-style slaw.
- Toss with sliced grilled or broiled skirt steak and serve in lettuce cups. Garnish with chopped peanuts and mint and serve with hot sauce, such as Srirachi.
- Mound onto grilled swordfish.

pistachio-herb

This pesto is woven together with different herbal accents making for a complex topping. The crunchy texture and concentrated flavor create a dynamic crust for pork chops or sea bass.

$^1/_2$ cup salted roasted pistachio nuts
2 tablespoons chopped fresh lemon thyme
3 tablespoons chopped fresh flat-leaf parsley
1 tablespoon chopped fresh tarragon
1 garlic clove, minced
$1^1/_2$ tablespoons fresh lemon juice
$^1/_4$ cup freshly grated Parmesan cheese
4 to 5 tablespoons olive oil

Place the nuts, thyme, parsley, tarragon, garlic, lemon juice, and cheese in the bowl of a food processor and pulse until a coarse mixture forms. With the machine running, gradually stream in the oil and blend until the pesto emulsifies.

makes about 1 cup

serving suggestions

- Generously spoon over grilled or roasted pork chops.
- For a simple salad, thin the pesto with more olive oil and spoon over thick slices of fresh heirloom tomatoes.
- Paddle a thick layer of this pesto onto sea bass or halibut and broil or bake.

tapenades

Richly flavored, dense, and packing a punch, these tapenades strike head on. Whether decadent and sweet, like the Date & Almond tapenade, or rustic and briny, like the Traditional tapenade, these recipes will awaken your taste buds.

Originally from the Provence region of France, a *tapenade* is a thick, coarse paste made with an olive and anchovy base, but with a little creative license, the variations are plentiful. For our purposes, "tapenade" refers to a wide range of ingredients with one common theme: They all have a thick, coarse consistency that falls somewhere between the texture of a salsa and a spread. While the natural fit is atop crostini, these mixtures are equally at home with many preparations, whether giving a new twist to sandwiches or adding texture and interest to pork tenderloin, potatoes, or polenta.

traditional

This traditional tapenade, with a combination of olives, capers, and anchovies will be a favorite for any olive lover and is a true classic and a versatile condiment. Because this tapenade packs quite a flavor punch, a little goes a long way!

One	10-ounce jar or can pitted kalamata (or other) olives, drained and rinsed
3 to 4	anchovy fillets
2	garlic cloves, minced
1½	tablespoons fresh lemon juice
2	teaspoons chopped fresh thyme
1	tablespoon capers, drained
2	tablespoons olive oil
	Freshly ground pepper

Place all the ingredients in the bowl of a food processor and pulse until a coarse mixture forms.

makes about 1 cup

(serving suggestions, next page)

serving suggestions

- Serve over grilled or baked chicken, swordfish, or sea bass and garnish with chopped tomatoes and basil.
- Add to a gourmet sandwich with sliced lamb and arugula.
- For a special salad, toss 1 to 2 tablespoons with fresh spinach leaves, lemon juice, olive oil, and feta cheese.
- Coat boiled, quartered potatoes and add olive oil and coarse salt.
- Use as a condiment for turkey burgers.

tapenade, take two

While this tapenade is bold, it is a smoother, creamier counterpart to the Traditional tapenade. It has a softer mouthfeel, a good counterpoint to the salty undertones. I love to put small dishes of this tapenade on the dinner table instead of butter.

1	cup pitted kalamata or French olives, drained and rinsed
½ to 1	tablespoon anchovy paste
1	tablespoon fresh lemon juice
1	large garlic clove, minced
3 to 4	tablespoons mayonnaise (light or regular)
1	tablespoon olive oil
	Freshly ground pepper

Place all the ingredients in the bowl of a food processor and blend until almost smooth.

makes about 1 cup

serving suggestions
- ❦ Slather on a freshly sliced baguette or crostini.
- ❦ Place inside an omelet with feta cheese and spinach.
- ❦ Use as a condiment on sandwiches or burgers.

citrus-olive

Mouth-tingling citrus melded with the other ingredients in this tapenade makes for a potpourri of flavors that fill the mouth with a bang.

1 1/2 cups pitted green olives

1 to 2 garlic cloves, minced

Zest of 1 orange

Zest of 1 lemon

2 teaspoons fresh lemon juice

1 tablespoon chopped fresh parsley
(flat-leaf or curly)

1/2 teaspoon chopped fresh rosemary

1/2 teaspoon fennel seeds

1 small dried red chile, crushed

2 to 3 tablespoons olive oil

Salt and freshly ground pepper

Place the olives, garlic, orange and lemon zests, lemon juice, parsley, rosemary, fennel seeds, and red chile in the bowl of a food processor and pulse until the mixture starts to come together. With the machine running, gradually stream in the oil and mix until a coarse paste is formed. Season with salt and pepper.

makes about 1 cup

serving suggestions

- Stuff under the skin of chicken breasts with feta cheese and bake.
- Drizzle lamb chops with orange juice and olive oil and season with salt and pepper. Grill and top with the tapenade.

feta-mint

This tapenade is reminiscent of a *fattoush* salad, a common Syrian and Lebanese dish using garden vegetables, pieces of pita, and many of the ingredients in this recipe.

One 7.7-ounce can pitted kalamata olives, drained and rinsed (approximately 1 1/4 cups)

1 large clove garlic, minced

1 1/2 cups packed fresh mint leaves

1/4 cup pine nuts

1/4 cup feta cheese

3 tablespoons olive oil

1 tablespoon fresh lemon juice

Freshly ground pepper

Place all the ingredients in the bowl of a food processor and pulse until a coarse mixture forms.

makes about 1 3/4 cups

serving suggestions

- Spoon over grilled chicken or lamb.
- Serve simply with breadsticks.
- Thin with more olive oil and lemon juice and use as a tasty salad dressing; serve with romaine lettuce, onion, cucumber, tomato, and crumbled pita crisps or croutons. Add more mint to taste.

smoky eggplant

Although there are a few additional steps for this recipe, the caramelized flavor of the eggplant is worth the added time. The oozing, roasted flavors blended with the cumin make for a beguiling smokiness. I often incorporate this recipe as part of a Middle Eastern–inspired meal, although it's also great with pasta.

1 medium to large eggplant (12 to 16 ounces)
2 tablespoons olive oil
   Salt and freshly ground pepper
1 clove garlic, minced
$1/3$ cup pitted kalamata olives, drained and rinsed
$1/2$ teaspoon ground cumin

Preheat the oven to 425 degrees F. Trim the ends off the eggplant, and cut it horizontally into 1-inch slices. Place the eggplant in a single layer on a baking sheet lined with aluminum foil and brush the slices with 1 tablespoon of the oil. Sprinkle with salt and pepper. Roast for 10 minutes, then flip the slices over and roast for 6 minutes more. Let cool slightly. Peel the slices, discard the peels, then place the eggplant flesh, garlic, olives, cumin, the remaining 1 tablespoon oil, and $1/8$ teaspoon salt in the bowl of a food processor. Blend until almost smooth.

makes about $1 1/2$ cups

serving suggestions

- Serve with pita crisps or put a thick layer on crostini.
- Use on a grilled vegetable sandwich.
- For a baked pasta dish, toss cooked pasta with the eggplant tapenade and ricotta cheese. Put the mixture into a baking dish, add a layer of canned diced tomatoes, and finish with slices of provolone or mozzarella cheese. Bake at 375 degrees F for 6 to 10 minutes.

roasted fennel

Roasting fennel softens and smooths out its wonderful anise flavor. When mixed with the creamy garlic and sweet onion, it makes a mild yet captivating tapenade.

$1\frac{1}{2}$ to 2 pounds fennel

$\frac{1}{2}$ sweet onion (such as Vidalia), quartered

3 to 4 large garlic cloves, unpeeled

4 tablespoons olive oil

1 teaspoon chopped fresh thyme

$\frac{1}{4}$ teaspoon salt

Freshly ground pepper

Preheat the oven to 400 degrees F. Cut the tops and bottoms off the fennel bulbs. Quarter the fennel bulbs, removing any remaining bits of hard core (you should have about 4 cups). Toss the fennel, onion, and garlic with 1 tablespoon of the oil. Place on a baking sheet lined with aluminum foil and roast for about 20 minutes, until soft. Let cool slightly. Squeeze the roasted garlic into the bowl of a food processor, discarding the skins. Add the fennel, onion, the remaining 3 tablespoons oil, the thyme, and salt. Season with pepper and blend until a coarse mixture forms.

makes about 2 cups

serving suggestions

- Spread on crostini and top with shaved Parmesan cheese.
- Serve as a sauce for sautéed white fish. Sauté sole, orange roughy, or other flaky white fish in butter. Add lemon and spoonfuls of the tapenade and heat through. Serve with additional lemon wedges.
- Top roasted chicken with thin slices of sautéed apple and dollops of the tapenade.

portobello mushroom & thyme

The earthy flavors of this recipe combine superbly for a hearty tapenade. I like to serve this in early fall when I'm eager for the spirited flavors that cooler seasons bring, but when I can still comfortably use the outdoor grill.

4 tablespoons olive oil

1 large chopped shallot (about 3 tablespoons)

1 medium garlic clove, minced

1 tablespoon chopped fresh thyme, or
$\frac{1}{2}$ teaspoon dried thyme

2 medium-sized portobello mushrooms
(about 7 ounces total), chopped

2 tablespoons balsamic vinegar

$\frac{1}{3}$ cup pitted kalamata olives,
drained and rinsed

Salt and freshly ground pepper

Heat 1 tablespoon of the oil over medium heat. Sauté the shallot, garlic, and thyme for 2 to 3 minutes. Add the mushrooms and vinegar and cover. Cook for 2 minutes, then uncover and continue cooking until the liquid is slightly reduced by about one-third. Transfer the mushroom mixture and the olives to the bowl of a food processor and pulse until the ingredients start to come together. With the machine running, gradually stream in the remaining 3 tablespoons oil and pulse until a coarse paste forms. Season with salt and pepper.

makes about 1 cup

serving suggestions

- Serve on crostini topped with shaved Parmesan or Pecorino cheese.
- Layer with roast beef and Havarti cheese on a sandwich or panini.
- Serve as a condiment for grilled steak; garnish with chopped fresh parsley and/or thyme.

beautiful beet

The eye-catching color alone makes this recipe worth whipping up!
Its sweet yet earthy flavors will surprise you.

1 1/2 cups chopped beets (about 8 ounces),
   roasted, steamed, or boiled (not canned)

1/2 cup chopped walnuts

2 tablespoons balsamic vinegar

1 tablespoon olive oil

1/2 teaspoon salt, plus more as needed

Freshly ground pepper

Place all the ingredients in the bowl of a food processor and
blend to a coarse but spreadable paste. Season with more salt
and pepper as desired.

makes about 1 1/3 cups

serving suggestions

- Spread over crostini with soft goat cheese.
- Dollop over spinach salad with goat cheese, balsamic vinegar, and olive oil.
- Smear on a roasted vegetable or turkey sandwich.

shrimp-olive

This tapenade marries the lively seafood flavors you might find in a ceviche (a citrus-marinated seafood salad found in many Latin American countries) with olives for an unexpected merging of flavors. Serve this as an appetizer or a salad on a hot summer day with cool margaritas, and you're sure to have a backyard hit.

3 to 4 tablespoons olive oil

2 cups fresh or frozen (thawed) shrimp, deveined, tails and shells removed

⅓ cup pitted kalamata olives, drained and minced

2 tablespoons chopped fresh flat-leaf parsley

1 tablespoon chopped green onions (whites and greens)

Juice of 1 lime

Juice of 1 small lemon

1 to 2 dried chile peppers, crumbled

¼ teaspoon salt

Freshly ground pepper

Heat 1 tablespoon of the oil over medium heat. Sauté the shrimp for 2 to 3 minutes. Drain any liquid from the pan. Transfer the shrimp to the bowl of a food processor. Add the olives, parsley, onions, lime and lemon juice, chile peppers, and salt, season with pepper, and pulse until a coarse mixture forms.

makes about 1 cup

(serving suggestions, next page)

serving suggestions

- Scoop up with crisp tortilla chips.
- For a fresh salad, spoon into avocado halves and squeeze with lime or lemon. Garnish with fresh parsley and/or finely chopped red bell pepper.
- Toss with ravioli and ricotta or soft goat cheese. Add diced red bell pepper and/or seeded, diced tomatoes.
- Place a tablespoonful on endive spears for a quick appetizer.

roasted red pepper

Roasted red peppers add big flavor without the heat of other varietals of peppers. This is an easy one to please the eye and the taste buds.

One	12-ounce jar roasted red peppers, drained (about 8 ounces of actual peppers)
1	garlic clove, minced
1	tablespoon chopped fresh parsley
1/3	cup pitted kalamata olives, drained and rinsed
2	teaspoons capers, drained
	Salt and freshly ground pepper

Place all the ingredients in the bowl of a food processor and pulse to a coarse mixture. Be careful not to purée to a smooth paste.

makes about 1 cup

serving suggestions

- Dollop over roasted or pan-fried fish
- Spoon over steamed green beans.
- Toss with sautéed spinach or kale.
- Slather on warm bread or crostini.

sun-dried tomato

Sun-dried tomatoes have a sweet, intense tomato flavor that concentrates the essence of everything that we love about fresh tomatoes. Their dense texture is perfect for this nutrient- and lycopene-rich tapenade.

$1/2$ cup oil-packed sun-dried tomatoes, drained

1 small garlic clove, chopped

$1/2$ cup pitted kalamata olives, drained and rinsed

2 tablespoons chopped fresh flat-leaf parsley

3 tablespoons chopped fresh basil

1 to 3 tablespoons olive oil

Salt

Place all the ingredients in the bowl of a food processor and pulse until a coarse paste forms. Add more oil as needed to thin.

makes $3/4$ to 1 cup

serving suggestions

- Serve over polenta squares and top with shaved Parmesan cheese. Garnish with ribbons of fresh basil.
- Toss with pasta and broccoli and top with cheese.
- Stir into scrambled eggs at the end of cooking.
- Top grilled or roasted meat, poultry, or fish.

balsamic fig & caramelized onion

With a subtle sweetness and jammy quality, this tapenade is great with grilled pork. If you like more sweetness, add the honey.

1 tablespoon olive oil, plus ⅓ cup
1 medium red onion, chopped
1 cup chopped Black Mission figs
¼ cup balsamic vinegar, plus 2 tablespoons
Salt and freshly ground pepper
1 to 2 teaspoons honey (optional)

Heat the 1 tablespoon oil over medium heat. Sauté the onion until soft and beginning to brown, about 4 minutes. Add the figs and the ¼ cup balsamic vinegar and continue to sauté until most of the liquid is gone and the mixture is slightly caramelized, 2 to 3 minutes. Transfer the fig mixture to the bowl of a food processor. Add the remaining 2 tablespoons vinegar, season with salt and pepper, and add the honey (if using). Pulse until the ingredients start to come together. With the machine running, gradually stream in the remaining ⅓ cup oil and pulse until a coarse paste forms.

makes about 1 ⅓ cups

serving suggestions

- Serve over grilled pork tenderloin, chicken, or duck.
- Spread a thick layer on crostini and top each toast with a teaspoon of blue cheese. Add a sprinkle of walnuts, if you like. Or, instead of the cheese, add a thin slice of cooked pork.
- Use as a condiment for a chicken panini.

dried cherry

Dried cherries have a tart-sweet flavor that is a nice change from the more commonly used dried cranberries. Because this is made with dried fruit, it's always easy to find the necessary ingredients, making it a perfect go-to recipe year-round. You will get variation in the tartness and sweetness of this recipe depending on the cherries you use. Adjust the amount of brown sugar accordingly.

4 tablespoons olive oil

3 tablespoons chopped shallots

1 cup dried cherries

5 tablespoons red wine vinegar

2 to 3 teaspoons brown sugar

1 teaspoon dried ground ginger

$\frac{1}{2}$ cup chopped pecans

1 teaspoon fresh lemon juice

Salt and freshly ground pepper

Heat 1 tablespoon of the oil over medium heat. Sauté the shallots until they begin to brown, 2 to 3 minutes. Add the cherries and 3 tablespoons of the vinegar and cook until softened. Turn the heat to low and add the brown sugar and ginger, stirring until the sugar is dissolved and well incorporated. Transfer the cherry mixture to the bowl of a food processor. Add the remaining 3 tablespoons oil, the remaining 2 tablespoons vinegar, the nuts, and lemon juice and blend until a thick paste forms. Season with salt and pepper. Add 1 or 2 tablespoons of water, as needed, to thin the tapenade to a spreadable consistency.

makes about 1 cup

serving suggestions

- Serve over pork tenderloin. Slather pork tenderloin with a mixture of grainy mustard, crushed garlic, and a little olive oil. Bake at 380 degrees F until cooked to your liking (approximately 25 minutes). Fan sliced pork on plates and serve with a generous spoonful of the tapenade.
- Use as a condiment on a roasted turkey sandwich.
- Coat thickly on crostini and top with Brie, goat cheese, or blue cheese.

date & almond

These two ingredients are a perfect match. Because of the sweetness, this recipe works equally well as an appetizer or as part of a cheese or dessert course.

    1 cup pitted dates (deglet noor or medjool)
    ½ cup unsalted almonds
    2 tablespoons balsamic vinegar
    2 tablespoons almond oil (canola or grapeseed
        oil will work, as well)
    1½ to 2 teaspoons fresh lemon juice
    1 to 3 tablespoons water

Place the dates, almonds, vinegar, oil, and lemon juice in the bowl of a food processor and mix until the ingredients start to bind together. Add the water, 1 tablespoon at a time, until a coarse paste forms. The tapenade will remain thick and a bit sticky.

makes about 1 cup

serving suggestions

- Smooth onto crostini and top each one with soft goat cheese, or Manchego cheese for a bigger bite.
- Split a wedge of Brie horizontally (creating a top and bottom). Using a spatula, coat the bottom layer of the Brie with the tapenade, then replace the top. Serve wedges of the cheese warm or at room temperature with baguette slices or crackers.
- Serve over roasted pork or turkey.
- As a dessert, spread on top of cookies (almond, shortbread, or vanilla) or warm a few tablespoons of the spread and paddle into vanilla ice cream.

spreads

These spreads are alternately dipped into and smoothed on. They are creamier in consistency than pestos and tapenades and are wonderful straight out of the bowl with your favorite chip or veggie. They are equally alluring over crostini, in sandwiches, and dolloped onto entrées as well. Ingredients such as cheese, yogurt, beans, or tofu are at the heart of many of the recipes in this chapter, offering great mouthfeel and heartiness that comfort and delight. While the spreads are velvety and feel sinful, you will find that many use light or nonfat alternatives that keep them from being overly weighed down. Setting out Curried Hummus or Avocado-Chèvre spread on your coffee table as guests arrive for a dinner party will surely satisfy early hunger, while Smoked Salmon spread is a wonderful addition to any holiday brunch. Once again, you will find an ease and adaptability that can't be beat!

curried hummus

In traditional hummus, we expect a mix of chickpeas, garlic, and olive oil. This recipe is a great alternative with the smoky-sweet flavors of curry and cumin. Adjust the amounts of lemon, garlic, and oil to suit your taste. The dried chile adds kick, so feel free to omit it, or turn it up a notch by adding more!

One	15-ounce can garbanzo beans (chickpeas), drained
1 to 2	garlic cloves, minced
1	small dried red chile pepper, crumbled
	Juice of 1 to 2 medium lemons
1/2	teaspoon ground cumin
1 1/2	teaspoons curry powder
6 to 7	tablespoons olive oil
	Salt and freshly ground pepper

Place the chickpeas, garlic, chile, lemon juice, cumin, and curry powder in the bowl of a food processor and blend until the mixture begins to bind together. With the machine running, gradually stream in the oil and blend until the oil is incorporated and the spread is almost smooth. Season with salt and pepper.

makes about 1 1/4 cups

serving suggestions

- Serve with baked pita crisps or crudités.
- Dollop over grilled vegetables.
- Spread in fresh pita pockets and add your favorite vegetables for a great sandwich.

edamame hummus

Edamame, fresh soybeans, are the base for this healthful yet tempting spread. For a fun evening, host a Japanese-inspired dinner party and prepare this recipe as an appetizer. Pickled ginger is available in the international food aisle of most grocery stores.

1 cup edamame, cooked and shelled
1 tablespoon tahini
1 tablespoon pickled ginger
Juice from 1 lime
Juice from 1 small lemon
3 to 4 tablespoons olive oil
$1/2$ to 1 dried chile pepper, crushed
Salt and freshly ground pepper

Place all the ingredients in the bowl of a food processor and blend until almost smooth.

makes about 1 cup

serving suggestions

- Serve with crudités.
- Use as a dip for cooked, cooled shrimp (for this preparation, add more oil and blend until smooth in the food processor).
- Spread on crostini topped with sliced seared ahi tuna.

white bean-sage

The velvety balance of flavors in this spread makes for a comforting recipe that evokes the hillsides of Tuscany. Using a full-bodied, rich olive oil enhances the flavor of the white beans.

4 tablespoons olive oil

4 tablespoons chopped fresh sage

3 garlic cloves, chopped

One 15-ounce can cannellini beans (white beans), drained and rinsed

4 teaspoons fresh lemon juice

$\frac{1}{2}$ teaspoon salt (kosher is preferable)

Freshly ground pepper

Heat 2 tablespoons of the oil over medium heat. Add the sage and garlic and sauté until very fragrant, 2 to 3 minutes. Transfer the sage mixture to the bowl of a food processor; add the beans, lemon juice, salt, and the remaining 2 tablespoons oil and blend until almost smooth. Season with pepper.

makes about 1 $\frac{1}{2}$ cups

serving suggestions

- Serve with pita crisps or crudités.
- Make a wrap. Spread onto flour tortillas, top with grilled vegetables, and roll it up.
- Generously top crostini and then sprinkle with crumbled bacon.

avocado-chèvre

I love guacamole, but wanted to come up with an alternative recipe for creamy avocados. I like that this spread is a snap to make and adds lively flavor to simple meals. When zesting lemons, make sure to zest just the yellow part, as the white pith will add unwanted bitterness.

2	medium avocados, split and flesh scooped out
One	5-ounce package of chèvre (soft goat cheese)
3	teaspoons lemon zest
4 to 5	teaspoons fresh lemon juice
1	garlic clove, minced
1/4	teaspoon salt
	Freshly ground pepper

Place the avocado, chèvre, lemon zest, lemon juice, garlic, and salt in the bowl of a food processor and blend until smooth. Season with pepper.

makes about 1 1/4 cups

serving suggestions

- Serve on crostini with fresh cracked pepper or cayenne pepper and shaved Parmesan cheese.
- Spread over sautéed or grilled ahi tuna or salmon. Dust with cayenne pepper. Serve with lemon wedges.
- Add to a vegetarian sandwich or a tuna sandwich.
- Serve as a dip for corn chips, pita chips, or veggies.

sun-dried tomato–chèvre cheese

This is a crowd-pleaser that's great to have on hand for a last-minute gathering. The vibrant orange hue adds festivity to any party. I serve this on Halloween with black-bean chips and blue-corn tortilla chips—the colors fit perfectly with the pumpkin and bat decorations!

$\frac{1}{2}$ **cup sour cream (light or regular)**

4 **ounces oil-marinated sun-dried tomatoes, drained**

1 to 2 **garlic cloves, minced**

4 **ounces chèvre (soft goat cheese)**

1 to 2 **tablespoons milk**

1 **tablespoon chopped fresh basil or chives**

Salt and freshly ground pepper

Place the sour cream, sun-dried tomatoes, garlic, and chèvre in the bowl of a food processor and mix until the ingredients start to come together. Gradually add the milk, as needed, until a creamy consistency forms. Fold in the basil. Season with salt and pepper.

makes about 1$\frac{1}{4}$ cups

serving suggestions

- Serve as a dip with tortilla chips and/or crudités.
- Use as a condiment in "roll ups." Slather on softened lavash bread or tortillas, add roast beef or turkey, then roll up and slice into pinwheels.
- Top broiled or poached fish such as snapper or halibut with this spread.
- Spoon over grilled steak.
- Sauté with sliced chicken breast (chicken tenders). Season the chicken with salt and pepper and sauté in a few tablespoons of olive oil. Once the chicken is browned, add the tomato spread to the pan and continue sautéing until the chicken is cooked through.

toasted pecan & gorgonzola

Toasting the pecans coaxes out their full nutty flavor, which layers well with the pungent taste of Gorgonzola cheese. My mom raves about using this spread as a topper for baked potatoes.

> 8 ounces whipped cream cheese
>   (light or regular)
> 1/2 cup Gorgonzola cheese
> 1/4 cup toasted pecans
> 2 tablespoons fresh lemon juice
> 1/4 cup chopped fresh chives
> 1/4 teaspoon freshly ground pepper
> 1/4 teaspoon powdered mustard

Place all the ingredients in the bowl of a food processor and pulse to combine. Be careful not to overblend as you still want small pieces of pecan to stud this spread.

makes about 1 cup

serving suggestions

- Slather on crusty baguette slices and top with thin slices of pear.
- Serve with crackers or cucumber slices.
- Smooth over grilled pork tenderloin.
- Mix with roasted butternut squash and cheese- or squash-filled ravioli.

creamy balsamic onion

This is like a refined, homemade version of the onion dips we used to see at every football party. Caramelizing the onion with balsamic vinegar adds a deep, malty flavor that really takes this to a new level.

1 tablespoon olive oil
1 cup diced sweet onion (such as Vidalia)
3 tablespoons balsamic vinegar
$\frac{1}{2}$ cup sour cream (light or regular)
4 ounces cream cheese, softened
$\frac{1}{2}$ teaspoon granulated or powdered garlic
Salt and freshly ground pepper

Heat the oil over medium heat. Sauté the onion until translucent and lightly browned. Remove from the heat and add the vinegar to the pan. In a medium bowl, combine the sour cream, cream cheese, and garlic, then fold in the onion mixture until well incorporated. Season generously with salt and pepper.

makes about 1$\frac{1}{2}$ cups

serving suggestions

- Set on a platter with thick-cut potato chips and/or crudités; for color, garnish with chives or parsley.
- Use as a dip for steamed artichokes.
- Heap onto baked potatoes.
- Use as a condiment for BLT sandwiches.

caesar

This has all of the lively flavors of your favorite Caesar salad!

    4 ounces whipped cream cheese
      (light or regular)
    1 garlic clove, minced
    1 tablespoon fresh lemon juice
    2 tablespoons mayonnaise (light or regular)
    3 tablespoons finely grated Parmesan cheese
$1/2$ to 1 tablespoon anchovy paste
    1 teaspoon Dijon mustard
    Salt and freshly ground pepper

Place the cream cheese, garlic, lemon juice, mayonnaise, Parmesan, anchovy paste, and mustard in the bowl of a food processor. Season with salt and pepper and blend until almost smooth.

makes about $1/2$ cup

serving suggestions

- Slather on crostini or hearty crackers with slices of smoked trout (or other smoked fish) and garnish with half of a cherry tomato.
- Serve with crudités or grilled vegetables.
- Spread on a chicken or turkey panini.
- Smear on bread as an alternative to mayonnaise to make a veggie sub with avocado, tomatoes, and sprouts.
- Dollop over baked, roasted, or boiled potatoes.
- Crown baked salmon and garnish with fresh chopped chives.

black bean & roasted tomato

This smoky spread has a South American flair. It updates the classic refried bean dip by using black beans and fire-roasted tomatoes for a new spin on an old favorite.

One 15-ounce can black beans, drained
and rinsed

³/₄ cup canned fire-roasted tomatoes, drained

1 garlic clove, chopped

I serrano or jalapeño pepper, seeded and
finely chopped

Juice of ¹/₂ lime

1 teaspoon chili powder

¹/₂ teaspoon ground cumin

1 tablespoon olive oil

¹/₂ teaspoon salt

Freshly ground pepper

Hot sauce such as Tapatio or Tabasco
(optional)

Place the beans, tomatoes, garlic, serrano, lime juice, chili powder, cumin, oil and salt in the bowl of a food processor. Season with pepper and hot sauce and blend until almost smooth.

makes about 1¹/₂ cups

serving suggestions

- Serve with tortilla chips.
- Use as a filling for tacos or add a layer to quesadillas.
- Spoon over rice.
- Slather a thick layer on a tortilla and top with chopped fresh lettuce, tomatoes, avocado, and cheese for a tostada. Serve with lime wedges.

rich crab

Seafood always seems to add elegance to a party. I keep a few cans of crabmeat on hand so that I can quickly make this recipe to dress up a last-minute event.

8 ounces cream cheese

10 to 12 ounces crabmeat (fresh or canned)

2 tablespoons mayonnaise

1 tablespoon chopped green onion (white and green parts)

2 1/2 tablespoons fresh lemon juice

1/2 cup finely diced celery

2 tablespoons seafood cocktail sauce

10 to 15 drops hot sauce such as Tapatio or Tabasco

1/4 teaspoon salt

Freshly ground pepper

Bring the cream cheese to room temperature or microwave until just soft. Drain the crab well, making sure to press out all the liquid. Place the cream cheese, crabmeat, mayonnaise, onion, lemon juice, celery, cocktail sauce, hot sauce, and salt in a bowl and season with pepper. Using a spatula, mix until well incorporated.

makes about 2 cups

serving suggestions

- Serve in endive leaves for a chilled appetizer.
- Put in a bowl alongside butter crackers.
- Fold into the center of an omelet.
- Use on top of toasted English muffins with poached eggs.

smoked salmon

Whether for a family brunch or an evening soirée, smoked salmon is always a sure bet. This spread marries the smoky-salty flavor of the fish with a natural partner, dill, and then gets a lift from the horseradish and lemon.

8 ounces cream cheese

$1/4$ cup plain yogurt (nonfat or low-fat)

4 ounces smoked salmon

$1 1/2$ tablespoons fresh lemon juice

$1 1/2$ tablespoons chopped fresh flat-leaf parsley

1 tablespoon chopped fresh dill

1 teaspoon prepared horseradish

2 to 3 tablespoons finely chopped red onion

Freshly ground pepper

Place the cream cheese, yogurt, salmon, lemon juice, 1 tablespoon of the parsley, the dill, and horseradish into the bowl of a food processor and blend until well incorporated and the spread is just starting to smooth out. Using a spatula, fold in the onion and the remaining $1/2$ tablespoon of parsley. Season with pepper.

makes about 2 cups

(serving suggestions, next page)

serving suggestions

- Serve with crackers, celery, or small triangles of rye bread.
- Smear thick layers on toasted bagels.
- Add to scrambled eggs or an omelet.
- Scoop out cherry tomatoes or cooked small red potatoes and fill with the salmon spread; garnish with chopped dill.
- Make tea sandwiches with thinly sliced cucumber and the spread.

savory tofu

This is a wonderful alternative to egg salad and offers a healthful, protein-packed option for vegetarians and vegans.

7 to 8 **ounces extra-firm tofu**

3 **tablespoons mayonnaise (eggless or regular)**

3 **teaspoons Dijon mustard**

2 to 3 **teaspoons apple cider vinegar**

1/4 **cup finely chopped celery**

1 **tablespoon finely chopped fresh chives**

1/2 **teaspoon sweet paprika**

1/4 **teaspoon salt**

Freshly ground pepper

Place the tofu, mayonnaise, mustard, and vinegar in the bowl of a food processor and blend until almost smooth. Using a spatula, fold in the celery, chives, paprika, and salt. Season with pepper.

makes about 1 1/4 cups

serving suggestions

- Spoon atop crackers.
- Spread onto white bread and cut into triangles, removing the crusts to create vegan tea sandwiches.
- Use in a sandwich with tomato, lettuce, and cucumber slices.
- For breakfast, smear onto toasted bagels.

tahini tofu

What is tahini? It's a paste like peanut butter except it's made with sesame seeds. Sesame and ginger are perfect partners in this snappy spread. I like to scoop it up using celery sticks for a simple, protein-rich snack.

7 to 8 ounces medium or regular tofu
(do not use extra-firm)
$1/3$ cup tahini
3 tablespoons seasoned rice wine vinegar
Juice from 1 lime
2 teaspoons peeled and grated ginger
$2 1/2$ teaspoons soy sauce (dark or light)
1 tablespoon chopped green onion
(greens only)

Place the tofu, tahini, vinegar, lime juice, ginger, and soy sauce in the bowl of a food processor and blend until smooth. Using a spatula, fold in the green onion.

makes about $1 1/2$ cups

serving suggestions

- Serve as a snack with celery sticks.
- Toss with Asian rice noodles or wheat noodles and stir-fried vegetables.
- Serve as a dip alongside sesame shrimp or chicken satay; garnish with green onion or chives.
- Swirl into rice and serve with a wedge of lime.

blueberry-cheese

While I mostly wanted to concentrate on savory spreads for this book, I had to include at least one recipe that satisfies my extreme sweet tooth! While this is sweet, it's not cloyingly so, which makes it perfect for breakfast dishes or light desserts. Ricotta cheese has a slightly grainy texture, which I love as a unique alternative to cream cheese-based spreads.

- $^3/_4$ cup ricotta cheese
- $^1/_2$ cup frozen (no sugar added) blueberries, thawed and drained
- 3 tablespoons powdered sugar
- 1 tablespoon sour cream (light or regular)
- $^1/_2$ teaspoon lemon zest
- 2 tablespoons fresh lemon juice

Place all the ingredients in a medium bowl. Using a large fork, mix until some of the berries are crushed and the other ingredients are well incorporated. (Note that this recipe will have a thinner consistency than most of the other spreads.)

makes about 1 cup

serving suggestions

- Ladle over fresh fruit or granola.
- Serve in individual bowls with lemon or vanilla cookies.
- Use as a filling for crepes or atop pancakes or waffles.
- Scoop a generous dollop onto angel food cake and sprinkle with fresh berries.
- For a kids' snack, serve as a dip with graham crackers.

index

table of equivalents

The exact equivalents in the following tables have been rounded for convenience.

liquid/dry measurements

U.S.	METRIC
1/4 teaspoon	1.25 milliliters
1/2 teaspoon	2.5 milliliters
1 teaspoon	5 milliliters
1 tablespoon (3 teaspoons)	15 milliliters
1 fluid ounce (2 tablespoons)	30 milliliters
1/4 cup	60 milliliters
1/3 cup	80 milliliters
1/2 cup	120 milliliters
1 cup	240 milliliters
1 pint (2 cups)	480 milliliters
1 quart (4 cups, 32 ounces)	960 milliliters
1 gallon (4 quarts)	3.84 liters
1 ounce (by weight)	28 grams
1 pound	448 grams
2.2 pounds	1 kilogram

lengths

U.S.	METRIC
1/8 inch	3 millimeters
1/4 inch	6 millimeters
1/2 inch	12 millimeters
1 inch	2.5 centimeters

oven temperatures

FAHRENHEIT	CELSIUS	GAS
250	120	1/2
275	140	1
300	150	2
325	160	3
350	180	4
375	190	5
400	200	6
425	220	7
450	230	8
475	240	9
500	260	10